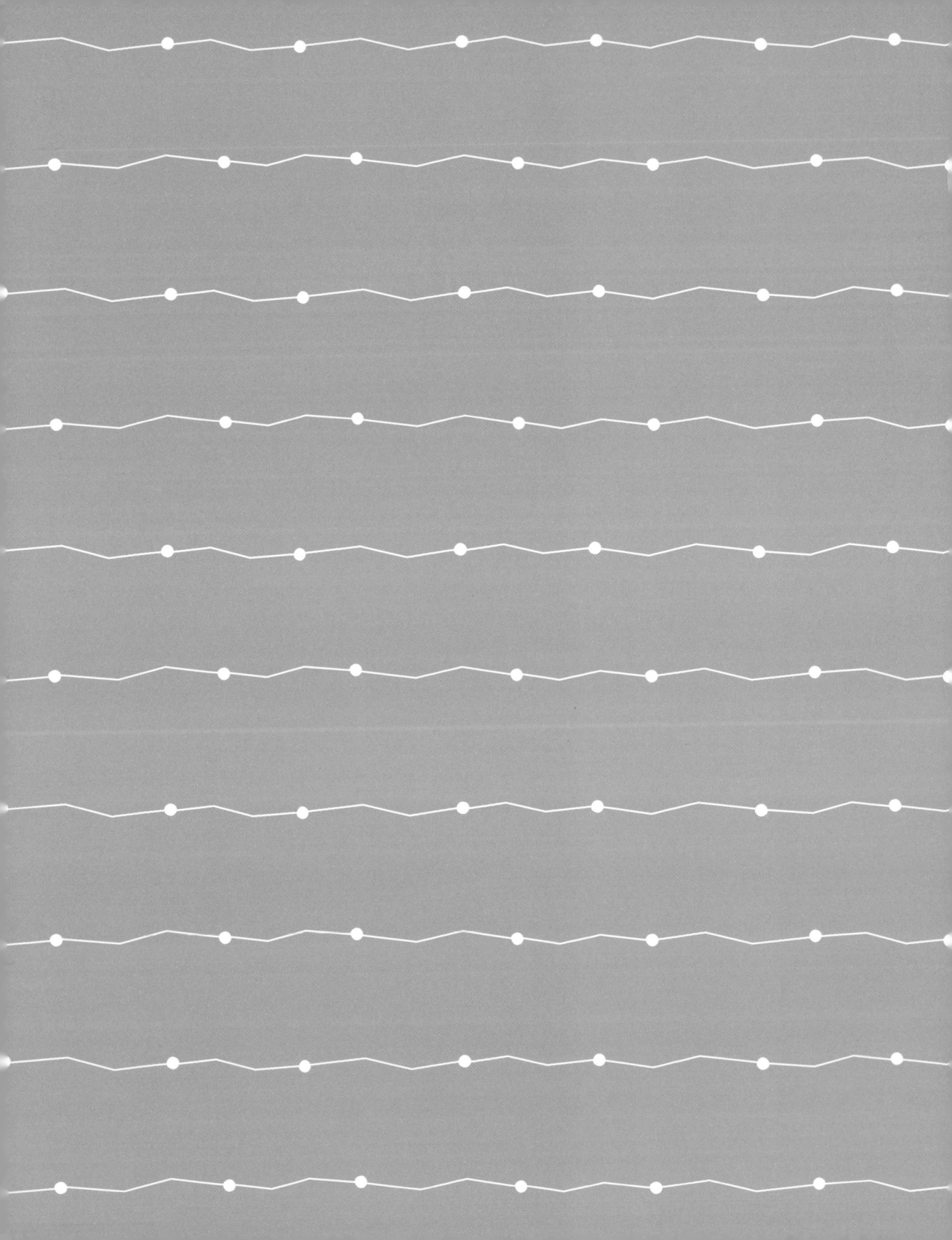

THE SCIENCE CLUB INVESTIGATES
ROCKS AND FOSSILS

By Mary Auld
Illustrated by Sernur Işik

The Science Club has a new project – rocks. Each child has brought something made of rock to the club.

Jack has an elephant statue.

Emily has a box of chalks.

It's for grinding spices.

Hazim has a small bowl.

Winston and Zoey have found some pebbles and stones.

Nadia thinks she's got the best rock of all.

"Look, I have a FOSSIL!"

"A fossil isn't a rock," says Liam. "It's an animal. Dinosaurs are fossils!"

"Fossils *are* rocks," says Mrs Khan. "They are traces of ancient plants or animals, like the dinosaurs, that have become part of the rock."

"So what is rock?" asks Nadia.

"Rock is the hard material that forms our Earth's crust," explains Mrs Khan. "There are many different types of rock. Look at what you have all found. And look at these!" She takes a cloth off the table. "Let's INVESTIGATE!"

Mrs Khan asks the children to do some tests on the rocks. They scratch them with a nail to decide how hard they are. Then they drop on a little water. Does it roll off or seem to bubble into the rock? The children carefully record their results.

Now Nadia has another question, "So why are there different types of rock?"

"Rocks are different because of the way they are made, but they are linked by the rock cycle," Mrs Khan says. "That's the name we give to the way rocks form and change over millions of years."

THE ROCK CYCLE

Rocks are made in different ways.

IGNEOUS rocks form above the ground when a volcano erupts, throwing up hot magma called lava.

IGNEOUS rock can form under the ground.

MAGMA

IGNEOUS rocks form when magma cools. Magma is molten rock, a superhot sludge found deep under the ground.

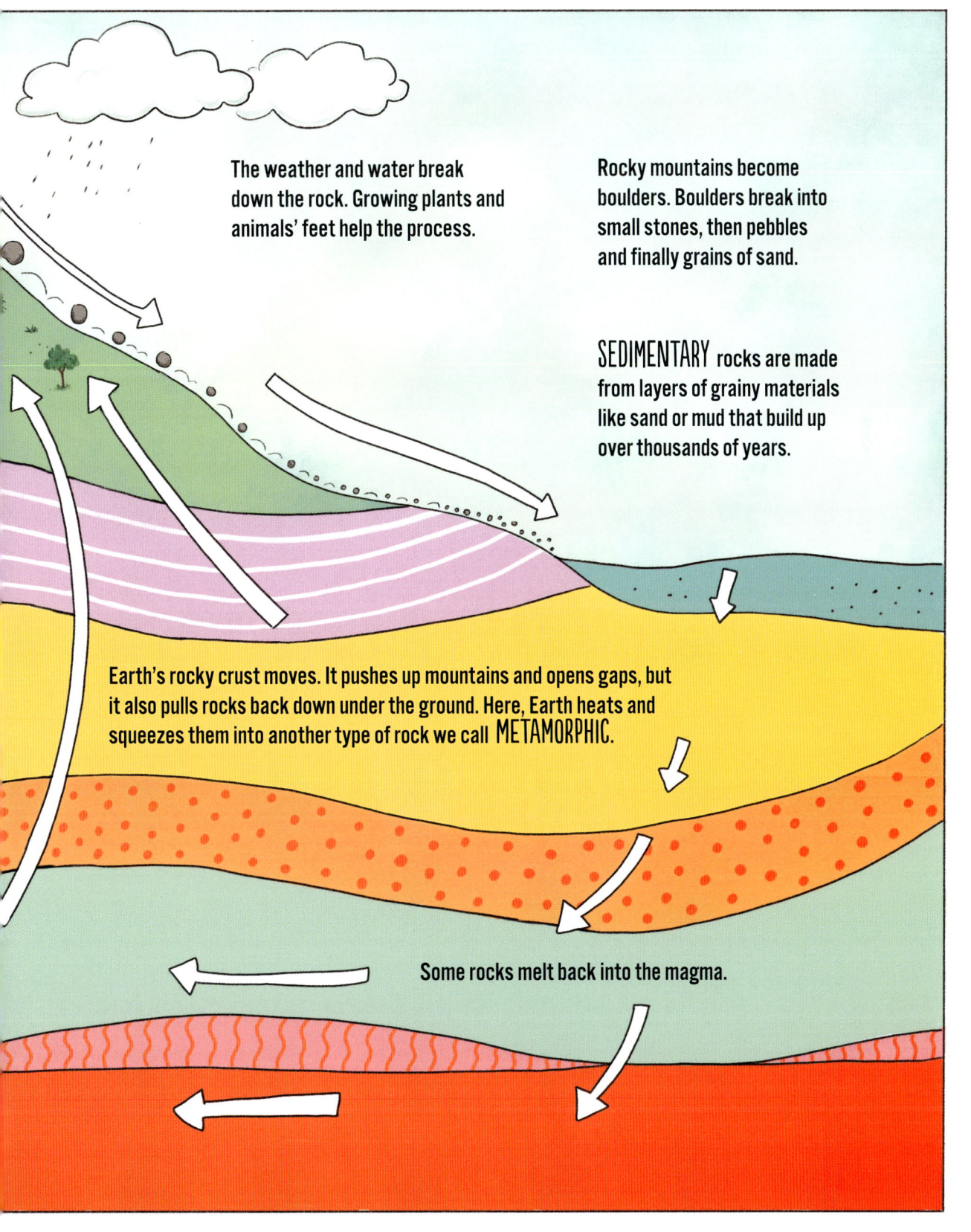

"Soil is part of the rock cycle, too," says Mrs Khan. "Let's INVESTIGATE!"
The Club go out to the school garden. They dig up samples of soil.

"Soil is made from worn-away rocks. The leaves rot into it and the worms help mix them up. It makes the soil good for growing things," says Mrs Khan.

The kids take their soil samples back inside. They look at them under the microscope. Nadia is excited. "I see tiny animals!"

"Those tiny animals might one day form fossils," says Mrs Khan. "We need to do some RESEARCH." She splits the club into four groups to look at the different types of rock – and fossils. Nadia and Liam will research fossils.

AT THE NEXT CLUB, the first group talk about igneous rock. "As magma cools it forms hard crystals locked together," begins Zoey. "The bigger the crystal grains, the slower the magma has cooled."

"When a volcano erupts, the magma cools really quickly. It forms rocks like basalt and pumice," says Hazim. "They have tiny crystals."

"Granite forms much more slowly. It cools deep underground," adds Ava. "Look, this sample has HUGE crystals."

"Granite moves to Earth's surface as the crust shifts. Here it is broken up and worn away over millions of years," explains Zoey. "Granite can eventually break down to form sand."

"Igneous rocks are very hard. A nail doesn't scratch them and water runs off them. They are good for building and paving – and for grinding spices!" adds Hazim, holding up his bowl.

Group two takes on sedimentary rocks. "They are made of sediment," says Jiang. "Sediment is sand and mud – and soil – that is made when rocks wear away. Sandstone is made of sand, mudstone is made of mud."

"Sedimentary rocks can also be made from the skeletons of tiny animals, like limestone," continues Emily, "or the build-up of dead plants – that's how coal forms."

"Sedimentary rocks are soft," says Winston. "A nail easily scratches them and water may drip through them. But we still build with them and use them to make other things – like concrete, glass and pottery."

Chalk's a type of limestone. It's so crumbly you can write and draw with it.

Jack holds up his statue. "My statue is carved marble. Marble is a metamorphic rock. It was once limestone – a sedimentary rock – that was pushed under the ground."

"It was squeezed and heated so much by Earth's heavy crust, it changed into a new kind of rock!" he adds. "That's how all metamorphic rocks are made."

Rocks are squashed underground by layers of rock on top.

"When can I talk about fossils?"

"Don't worry! You're next."

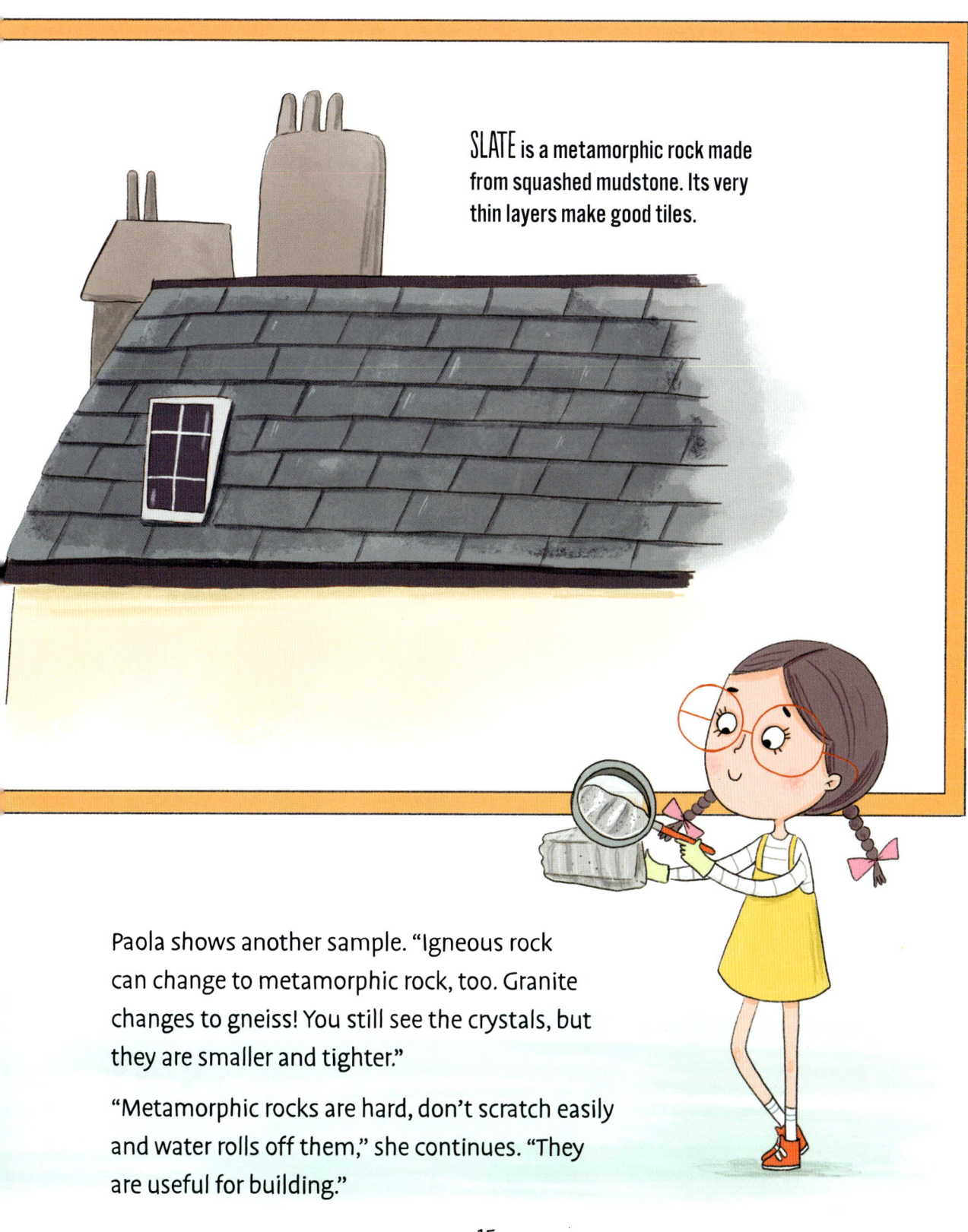

SLATE is a metamorphic rock made from squashed mudstone. Its very thin layers make good tiles.

Paola shows another sample. "Igneous rock can change to metamorphic rock, too. Granite changes to gneiss! You still see the crystals, but they are smaller and tighter."

"Metamorphic rocks are hard, don't scratch easily and water rolls off them," she continues. "They are useful for building."

It's Nadia and Liam's turn. "My fossil was an animal called an ammonite," begins Nadia. "It lived in the sea millions of years ago. When it died, it sank to the seabed and was covered with sand."

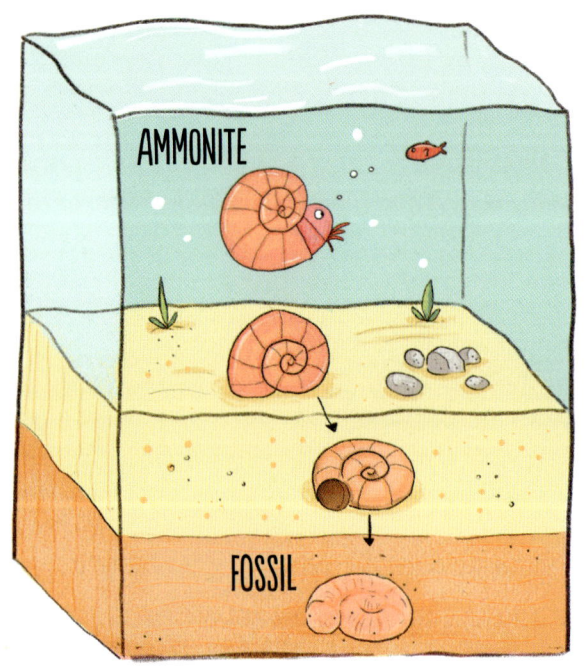

"This sand slowly became sandstone around the ammonite's hard shell," continues Liam. "The shell disappeared but another type of stone formed inside the shape it left. This is the fossil."

"Eventually, the sandstone became part of the land, then wore away to form a cliff – next to where me and my dad found it!" says Nadia proudly.

"Millions of fossils formed from sea animals," says Liam. "But sometimes land animals got buried by sand or mud – and their bones got fossilised too. That's how we know about the dinosaurs!"

Dinosaur is buried by mud.

Its bones become fossils.

"Fossils tell us about the animals and plants that lived on Earth millions of years ago. Long before humans existed!"

AT THE NEXT MEETING, Mrs Khan announces:

"We are going to be fossil hunters!"

"Like Mary Anning?" asks Nadia. She shares a book with the class.

Before the 1700s, people thought larger fossils were the remains of giants or dragons.

Then scientists, such as Henry De la Beche (1796–1855) and Mary Anning (1799–1847), realised they were the fossilised bones of extinct animals. They called the land animals 'dinosaurs', which means 'terrible lizards'.

"She found fossils in the cliffs like my dad and I did. She was one of the first palaeontologists – people who study fossils. I want to be like her!"

Mary found ancient sea reptiles, too, such as *plesiosaurus*. She sent sketches to other palaeontologists of the fossils she found.

"People have found fossils in sedimentary rock all over the world," says Mrs Khan. "Palaeontologists date the fossils by what layer of rock they found them in. They study the fossils to see what ancient life looked like."

"The map shows some of their finds. Let's imagine we are fossil hunters in Liaoning, China," she suggests.

TYRANNOSAURUS REX
(Montana, USA)

NORTH AMERICA

DIPLODOCUS
(Colorado, USA)

SOUTH AMERICA

GIGANOTOSAURUS
(Argentina)

The kids set out on their virtual hunt in Liaoning. "The life here was buried quickly in mud and volcanic ash," explains Mrs Khan. "It preserved things like feathers and flowers that usually rot away. We can even work out some of the colours."

The Club finds fossils big and small – not just of dinosaurs but of plants, fish, mammals, reptiles and birds.

They talk about their discoveries – including that dinosaurs had feathers.

Liam chips in: "I read that about 66 million years ago a large asteroid hit Earth! The huge explosion filled the air with dust. The big dinosaurs became extinct."

"But finds like the fossil of *Sinosauropteryx* helped palaeontologists work out something amazing," adds Nadia. "The birds on Earth today are relatives of the dinosaurs."

Not all the dinosaurs died out.

The Club decide to make a classroom display.

"We can have a rock cycle corner," suggests Hazim.

"And a rock and fossil museum," suggests Paola.

"We've got pictures," says Nadia, "and we can use my fossil in the display."

"How about we make some more fossils?" suggests Mrs Khan.

"Let's INVESTIGATE!"

Mrs Khan shows the Club how to make fossil models with clay. "These aren't like fossilised bones, but more like fossilised footprints or leafprints," she explains. "Some fossils are actually marks like this, made in sand or mud, that have become part of the rock. We call them trace fossils."

The kids proudly show off their display as people come to pick them up.

Nadia can't wait for her dad to see their fossil alongside the other rock samples. "Our ammonite," she tells him proudly, "comes from the same time as Tyrannosaurus Rex."

Everyone agrees that the rocks and fossils project has been brilliant.
"Rocks really rock!" laughs Hazim.

JOIN THE SCIENCE CLUB

INVESTIGATE rocks with this test (see page 5). You will need: a selection of rock samples (usually available in a starter geology set), an iron nail, water and a pipette. Protect your eyes with clear plastic goggles.

1. Try scratching each of your rock samples, first with your fingernail and then with the iron nail. What kind of mark do you make? Make a record of your results.

2. The harder the rock, the more difficult it is to scratch. Sort your samples from hardest to softest. What do you notice about the different types of rock?

3. Next, see if each rock sample is permeable (whether water can pass through it). Put a few drops of water from the pipette onto a sample. If the water bubbles and seems to disappear, the rock is permeable. Again, make a record of your results.

4. Rocks are permeable if there are gaps between the tiny grains or crystals that they are made of. How do your results compare with the Club's? What does this tell you about sedimentary rocks?

INVESTIGATE trace fossils with this activity (see page 25). You will need: air-drying clay, a rolling pin, some different shaped leaves, and hands and feet!

1. Research trace fossils on the Internet. Look for dinosaur footprints or the imprints of ferns (a type of plant). Now use clay to explore how the ancient marks were made.

2. Roll out some clay on a flat surface or tray.

3. Press your leaves into the clay so they lie flat in it. Carefully peel them off so you can clearly see their shape left in the clay. Leave the clay to dry.

4. Roll out some more clay and this time push your bare hands or feet into the surface. Carefully lift them out. Wash your hands and feet while the clay dries.

5. Make a display of your trace fossils.

GLOSSARY

asteroid	A rock in space that travels round the Sun. Asteroids can be big or small
crust	The hard, outer surface of Earth
crystals	Regular shaped, hard materials found in some rocks
dinosaur	A group of reptiles that lived on Earth between 245 and 66 million years ago
extinct	When a type of life has died out completely
fish	A group of animals with a backbone and fins that live underwater
fossil	A mark or remains of ancient life that has become part of rock
igneous rock	Rock that forms when magma cools and hardens, both under the ground and when a volcano erupts
magma	Super-hot, melted or molten rock found under Earth's crust
mammal	A group of animals with backbones that have fur or hair and feed their young on their milk. Humans are mammals
metamorphic rock	Rock made from other rock that has been squashed or heated under the ground
microscope	A device that makes tiny things look larger so we can see them more clearly
palaeontologists	Scientists who study ancient life, particularly through fossils
preserved	Kept like it was in the first place
reptile	A group of animals with backbones with dry, scaly skin. They lay eggs on land. Snakes and lizards are reptiles, as were dinosaurs
rock	The hard materials that form Earth's crust. There are different types of rock, grouped by the way they are made
rock cycle	The name given to the way rock changes from one form to another through natural processes over millions of years
sediment	Fine powder or material that is carried in water and then settles at the bottom, such as sand or mud
sedimentary rock	Rock made from the build-up of layers of sediment, often on the ocean floor
soil	The loose layer of materials on the Earth's surface where plants grow. It includes tiny pieces of rock and the remains of dead plants and animals

trace fossil   The type of fossil made when a life form leaves a mark in the ground, such as a footprint or a burrow

volcano   An opening in Earth's crust, often in the form of a mountain. When a volcano erupts, magma from beneath the crust comes out of it

FURTHER INFORMATION

Here are some other books about rock and fossils you might like to read:

Ultimate Rockopedia: The Most Complete Rocks and Minerals Ever (National Geographic Kids, 2020)

Eyewitness Activity: Rock and Fossil Hunter by Ben Morgan (DK, 2015)

Little People, Big Dreams: Mary Anning by Maria Isabel Sánchez Vegara (Frances Lincoln Books, 2021)

Dinosaur Infosaurus (series) by Katie Woolley (Wayland, 2019)

Check out these websites:

www.bbc.co.uk/bitesize/topics/z9bbkqt/articles/zsgkdmn
Start with this 'What is a rock?' section and follow links to fossils and soil.

kids.nationalgeographic.com/animals/prehistoric
This site is packed with information about dinosaurs and other prehistoric animals.

WARNING

Search 'fossil hunting' on the web to find places to hunt for fossils but you MUST go with an adult. Do not climb up cliffs and only take rocks if it is safe and allowed. Wear protective goggles. Most fossil-rich sites, such as the Jurassic Coast in the UK, have fossil-hunting rules – follow these.

SAFETY PRECAUTIONS

Always work with an adult while doing the investigations in this book. Be careful handling anything sharp. Ask an adult for help with difficult cutting and check any clay you use is safe for children. Clear up after you have finished, being careful to wash off any clay dust from your skin.

INDEX

ammonites 16,
animals 3, 7, 9, 12, 16, 17, 18
Anning, Mary 18
asteroids 23

basalt 4, 10
birds 22, 23
boulders 7, 11

chalk 2, 4, 13
clay 25, 29
cliffs 16, 19
coal 4, 12
crust 4, 7, 11, 14
crystals 10, 15, 28

De La Beche, Henry 18
dinosaurs 3, 17, 18, 22, 23

Earth 4, 7, 11, 14, 17, 23

fish 22

gneiss 4, 15
granite 4, 10, 11, 15

igneous rocks 6, 10, 11, 15

limestone 12, 13, 14

magma 6, 7, 10
mammals 22
marble 4
metamorphic rocks 7, 14, 15
microscopes 9
mud 7, 12, 17, 22, 25

nails 5, 11, 13, 28

palaeontologists 19, 20, 23
pebbles 2, 7, 11
plants 3, 7, 12, 17, 22, 29
pumice 4, 10

reptiles 19, 22
rock cycle 6, 8, 24

samples 8, 9, 10, 15, 26, 28
sand 7, 11, 12, 16, 17, 25
sandstone 4, 12, 16
sea 16, 17, 19
sediment 12
sedimentary rocks 7, 12, 13, 14, 20, 28
skeletons 12
slate 15
soil 8, 9, 12
stones 2, 7

trace fossils 25, 29

volcanos 6, 10

water 5, 7, 11, 13, 15, 16, 28
weather 7

First published in Great Britain in 2025 by Wayland
Copyright © Hodder and Stoughton, 2025
All rights reserved.

Wayland, an imprint of Hachette Children's Group
Part of Hodder and Stoughton
Carmelite House, 50 Victoria Embankment, London EC4Y 0DZ
An Hachette UK Company
www.hachette.co.uk   www.hachettechildrens.co.uk

HB ISBN: 978 1 5263 2104 6
PB ISBN: 978 1 5263 2105 3

Design by Clare Mills. Edited by Julia Bird and Rachel Cooke
Science consultancy by Peter Riley

Printed in China
The authorised representative in the EEA is Hachette Ireland, 8 Castlecourt Centre, Dublin 15, D15 XTP3, Ireland (email: info@hbgi.ie)

Note to parents and teachers: every effort has been made by the Publishers to ensure websites are suitable for children, that they are of the highest educational value, and that they contain no inappropriate or offensive material. However, because of the nature of the Internet, it is impossible to guarantee that the contents of these sites will not be altered. We strongly advise that Internet access is supervised by a responsible adult.

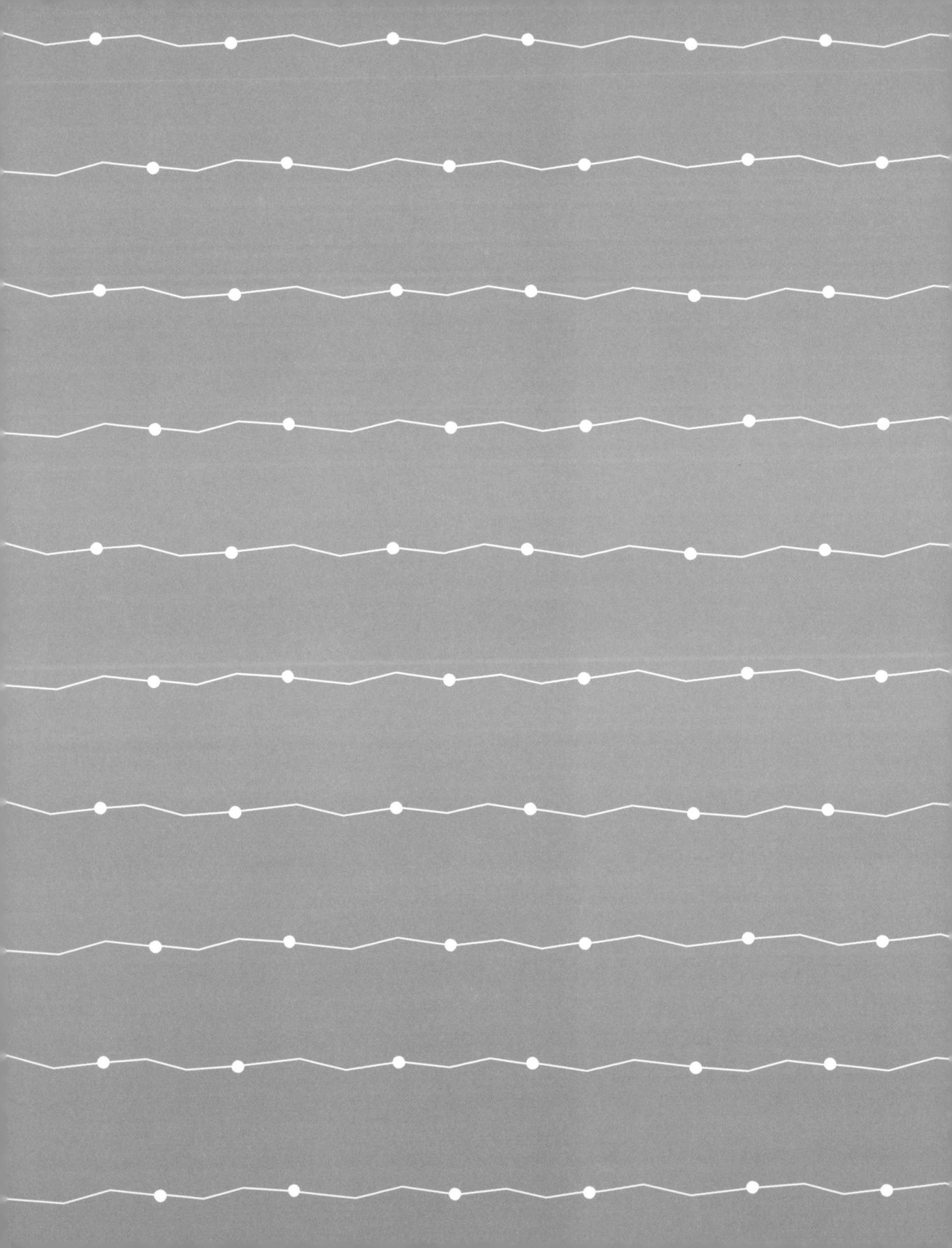